BRICK STITCH IN

Basic Rules for Angel Patterns

1. Read all material and check supplies before beginning.
2. You will not tie knots. To end or start new threads you will weave; in, out, back & forth, beads until thread is secure. Thread should not be showing between or over beads. Then thread may be cut.
3. I try to start with enough thread so I don't have to add, but sometimes plans fall through. Usually 1/2 for top section and 1/2 for the bottom section. Thread is not doubled.
4. Put your pattern into a clear protective sheet and use an erasable marker to keep track of where you are, you can reuse patterns again & again.
5. The use of wax or thread conditioners is optional; these products make your thread easier to handle (among other things). Wax is optional on small projects but required on larger ones. Anything thread can find to wrap around, including itself, it will.
6. Patterns are read in a zigzag fashion. Base row(s)=left to right, row 2=right to left, row 3=left to right, etc. Sometimes you will need to turn the pattern upside down to see your beginning triangle.
7. Instructions are written from a right hander's point of view. I hold the beads between my left thumb and forefinger and the needle in my right hand. I always work from left to right (reading pattern is still read in a zigzag fashion.) You will have to adjust your direction if you hold work other than described.

Up: the needlepoint is pointing in the up direction.

Down: needlepoint is pointing in the down direction.

Circle stitch example: Thread is coming out of the top of a bead: Pick up one bead, insert needle up through the bead the thread is coming out of, snug. Insert needle down bead just added.

2 Bead Base Row Technique

2 rows of beads at a time, faster for Delica or seed bead base rows.

Do not let go of the triangle made in step 1 while adding the 2 beads in step 2.

Only snug beads after the second stitch in step 2 is completed.

To snug the beads, pull the thread up and slightly to the left.

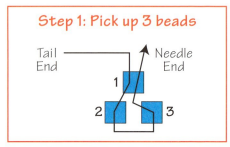

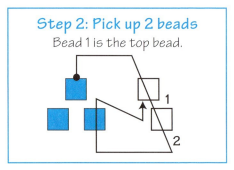
Bead 1 is the top bead.

Step 1: Read pattern left to right for base row. Pick up 3 beads, insert needle into bead 1 to form a triangle as shown. Use thumb and forefinger to hold these beads in place while doing step 2, if you let go 99% of the time you must just start over.

Step 2: This is a 2 stitch process do not snug bead until the second stitch is completed.

1st stitch of step 2: Pick up 2 beads, (1st bead picked up is the top bead), keep thread in back of needle and insert needle up into bead 3 of the triangle, pull gently.

2nd stitch of step 2: With thread in front of the needle, insert needle up into bead 1 just added and snug up, you should have 2 beads on top and 3 beads on bottom. (You can let go of the triangle now.)

Repeat step 2 to the end of the base row.

Complete base row before beginning Brick stitch section.

Row 2 - read pattern right to left. Make sure you are watching your pattern for correct color placement.

Brick Stitch:

1. Pick up 2 beads, insert needle under the loop of thread between beads, skip loop 1. Insert needle under loop 2 (needle pointing toward you (going from back to front)). Snug beads and thread.

Stitch shown: Green - red - blue.

(⌒ = Loops)

Insert needle up through the last bead added, (bead not on the end), snug up, this will make it stand on end.   * Insert needle down through the 1st of the 2 beads added (bead on the end) and back up through the 2nd bead (bead not on the end),* Your thread is coming out of the 2nd bead ready to add the third), * to* = a circle stitch.

(Thread is shown in Blue)

Snug beads into place. Both beads should stand on end and be secure.

2. Pick up 1 bead, insert needle under next loop. Snug gently. Insert needle up through the bead just added and snug. (Too tight and work is rigid, too loose and work is sloppy.)

3. Repeat step 2 to the end.

If your thread is pulled too tightly your work will become very rigid and many times warped. Try to relax, just pull up slack without yanking. Your completed work will be more flexible and smoother to the touch. This is very important.

Continue using the steps above for the brick stitch.

Increase & Decrease

Increasing - beginning of row:

Pick up 2 beads as always at the beginning of the row. Instead of inserting needle under the second loop of thread you will insert needle under 1st loop of thread, and snug. Insert needle up through the last bead added and snug, (1st bead added with shift left and be your increase). Insert needle down through the 1st of the 2 beads added and back up through the 2nd bead (you are just doing a circle stitch around the two beads, you will be coming out of the 2nd bead ready to add the third).

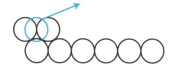

- To increase more than one bead at the beginning of the row: do steps shown above, then use the circle stitch.

Increasing - end of row:

When all beads are added for this row except the increase beads: your thread will be coming out of the last bead added: Add 1 bead, go up through the last bead added and snug, insert needle down into the bead to the left of the bead your thread is coming out of, snug. Insert needle into a bead in the row below at an angle, snug. Insert needle up one bead to the right of bead thread is coming out of and up into row above and out of bead just increased. (Its like a maze you must weave through beads so your thread doesn't show to get where you want to be - ready for the next bead.)

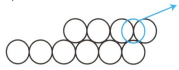

- To increase more than one bead at the end of the row: use the circle stitch.

Decreasing - Beginning of Row:

Example: Your thread is coming out of bead **1**; you must reposition the thread to be coming out of bead **2**. Insert needle down into bead **2**, down into bead in row below (bead **2**), up into bead on the side (bead **3**) (also in row below), and up into bead **2** of top row. Plan your route before starting, it is difficult to take out this thread. Add 2 beads at the beginning of your row as usual.

Decreasing - End of Row: Stop and turn to start next row, and/or, Position needle coming out of desired bead.

Finishing Work:

I have made these into pins for this book, but I have also made them into necklaces, and earrings.

Basically, follow the instructions for the AF1 angel to make them into pins.

You will have to use your imagination to make them into earrings or necklaces.

Have fun!

Angel #AF1

©1998 Rita Sova

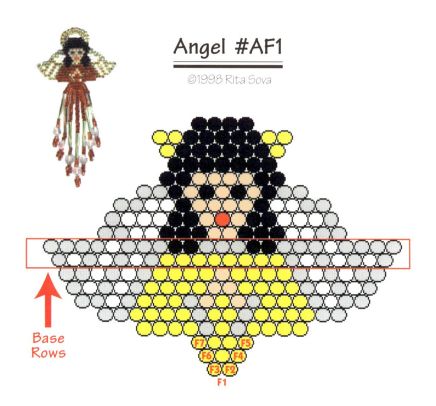

HALO: Add the halo as follows: Using the 2 gold beads sitting side by side in the hair section, position needle coming out one of inside gold beads, pick up 10 gold beads, insert needle into the gold bead on the opposite side of head (forming a half circle). Insert needle up through the gold edge bead next to the bead your thread is coming out of (ready for second row of halo). * Pick up 1 gold bead, insert needle into the last gold bead added for 1st row of halo (this is a circle stitch- no thread should go across beads. Insert needle back through the bead you just added on (you are ready to add next bead for row 2 of halo). * = Circle stitch. Continue the circle stitch moving around the halo until row 2 is completed. Secure halo to the opposite side. Weave your thread in to secure and cut. Add fringe after all brick stitch & halo is completed. Use the tail thread left when completing the bottom half of angel section.

FRINGE:

Your thread should be coming out of bead Marked F2. ***Whichever bead you want the fringe to hang from-your thread must be coming out of the bottom of that bead. Optional: For more of a V fringe affect use numbers in (). This fringe is also longer.

F1 Fringe: 1st fringe is the bottom center fringe. Pick up 10(16)-dress color beads, 1 bugle bead, 2(3)-dress color, 1-3mm, 3(5)-dress color beads. Insert needle up through all beads just added except the last 3(5) dress color beads - these are your turn around beads, and bead F3. Snug up pulling all excess thread to form fringe. Insert needle down out of bead F2.

Fringe F2 and F3: *pick up 8(12)-dress color beads, 1 bugle, 2(3)-dress color beads, 1-3mm, 3(5) dress color beads. Insert needle back up through all beads just added except last 3(5) turn around beads (3(5) beads create a small circle). * Insert needle into bead marked F2, repeat * to * using F3 instead of F2, then insert needle up 1 row and down out of bead marked F4.

PATTERN: F1: 10 (16)-dress color, 1 bugle, 2 (3) - dress color, 1-3mm, 3 (5)-dress color.

           F2 & F3: 8 (12)-dress color, 1 bugle, 2 (3) - dress color, 1-3mm, 3 (5)-dress color.

           F4 & F6: 6 (8)-dress color, 1 bugle, 2 (3) - dress color, 1-3mm, 3 (5)-dress color.

Angel #AF2

©1998 Rita Sova

Base Rows

Fringe

Use beads or replace with a Bugle bead for 6 yellow shown.

4mm bead.

3 to 5 bead turnaround.

8

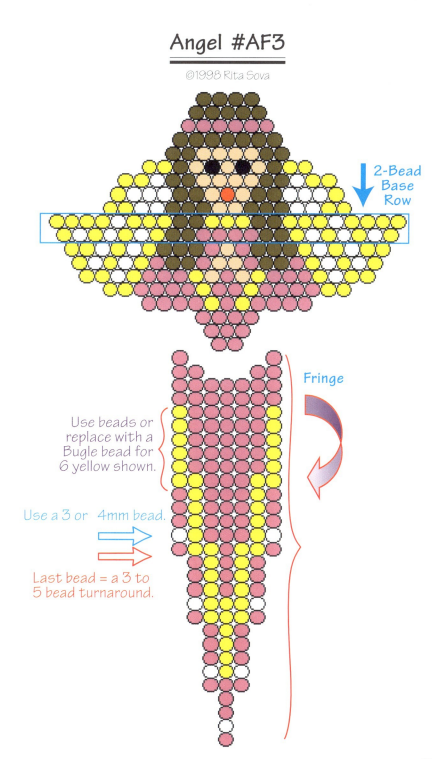

Angel #AF4

©1998 Rita Sova

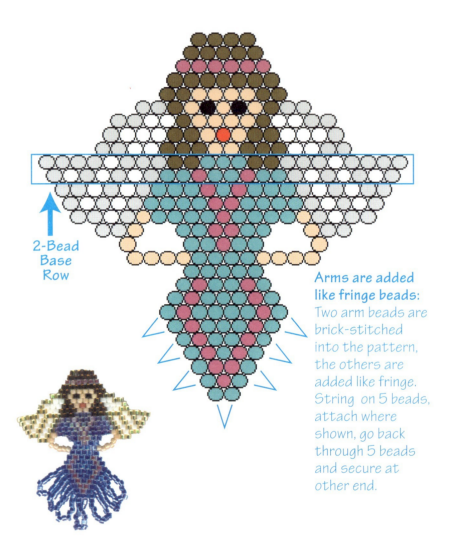

2-Bead Base Row

Arms are added like fringe beads: Two arm beads are brick-stitched into the pattern, the others are added like fringe. String on 5 beads, attach where shown, go back through 5 beads and secure at other end.

Fringe may be added to the dress bottom. I like a 15-bead loop for each > shown above (7 fringe). Thread is coming down out of a bead, add 15 beads, go up the bead shown grouped with the first bead. Repeat until all 7 fringe are added.

Angel #AF5

©1998 Rita Sova

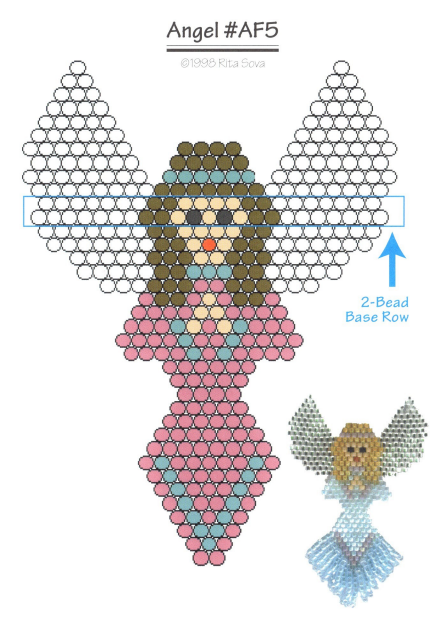

2-Bead Base Row

Fringe may be added to the dress bottom. I like a 16-bead loop from the bottom center (down bead on right, add 16 beads, go up 1st of 16 added and bead on left). A 15-bead loop from each of the remaining 16 beads forming the bottom V. Out one bead, up the same bead after fringe beads are added.

Angel #AF6

©1998 Rita Sova

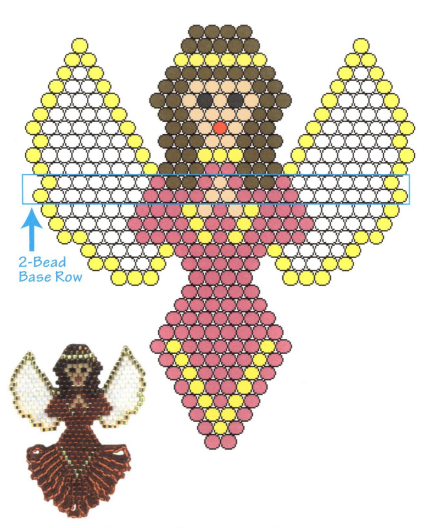

Fringe may be added to the dress bottom. I like a 16-bead loop from the bottom center (down bead on right, add 16 beads, go up 1st of 16 added and bead on left). A 15-bead loop from each of the remaining 16 beads forming the bottom V. Out one bead, up the same bead after fringe beads are added.

Angel #AF7

©1998 Rita Sova

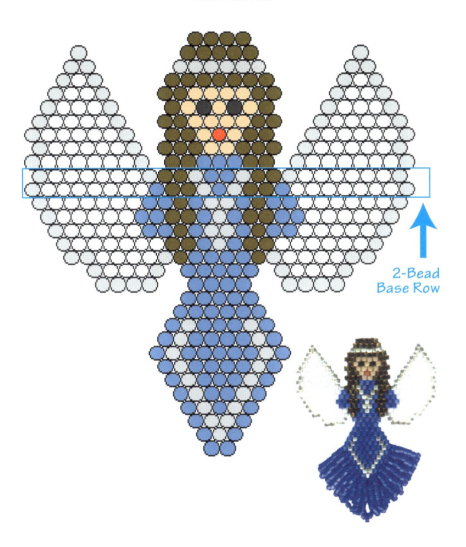

2-Bead Base Row

Fringe may be added to the dress bottom. I like a 16-bead loop from the bottom center (down bead on right, add 16 beads, go up 1st of 16 added and bead on left). A 15-bead loop from each of the remaining 16 beads forming the bottom V. Out one bead, up the same bead after fringe beads are added.

Angel #AF8

©1998 Rita Sova

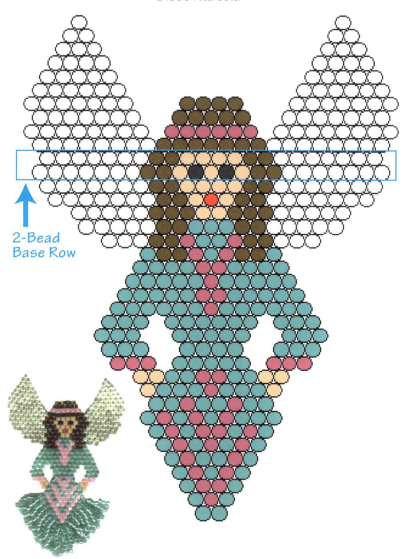

2-Bead Base Row

Fringe may be added to the dress bottom. I like a 16-bead loop from the bottom center (down bead on right, add 16 beads, go up 1st of 16 added and bead on left). A 15-bead loop from each of the remaining 16 beads forming the bottom V. Out one bead, up the same bead after fringe beads are added.

Angel #AF9

©1998 Rita Sova

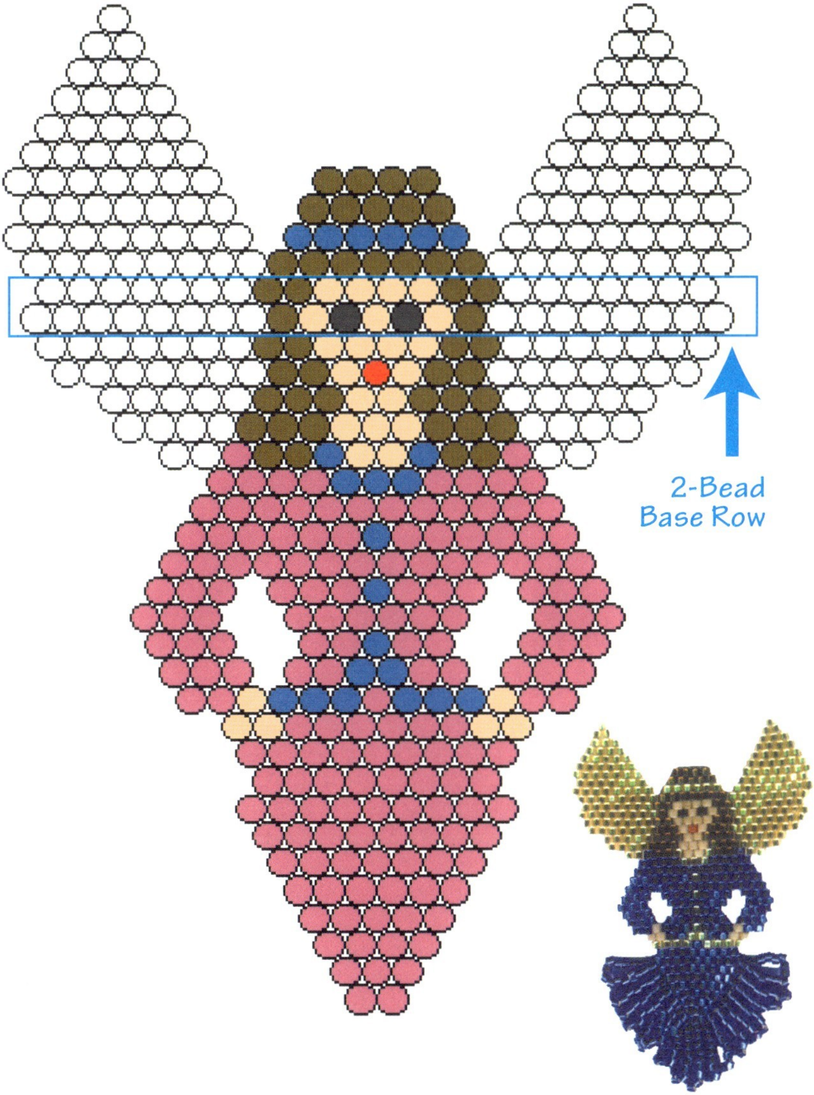

2-Bead Base Row

Fringe may be added to the dress bottom. I like a 16-bead loop from the bottom center (down bead on right, add 16 beads, go up 1st of 16 added and bead on left). A 15-bead loop from each of the remaining 16 beads forming the bottom V. Out one bead, up the same bead after fringe beads are added.

15

Angel #AF10

©1998 Rita Sova

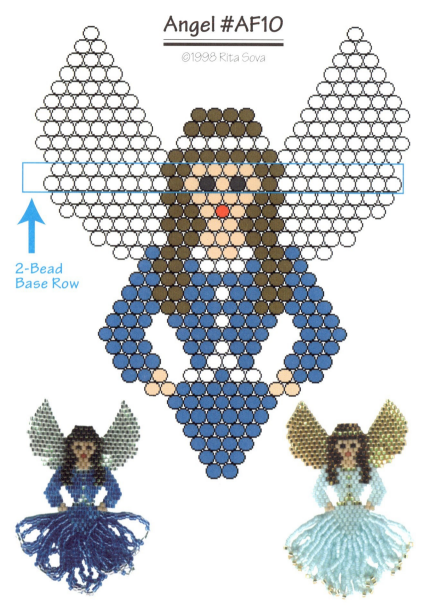

2-Bead Base Row

Fringe may be added to the dress bottom. I used: Start bottom center: 15 blue, 1 white, 1 blue,1white 14 blue (thread coming down bead on right, add 15-1-1-1-14, go up 1st bead added and bead on left), Repeat for remaining 12 V beads except insert needle through first bead added for fringe and back into same bead on the brick-stitch section.

Angel #AF11
©1998 Rita Sova

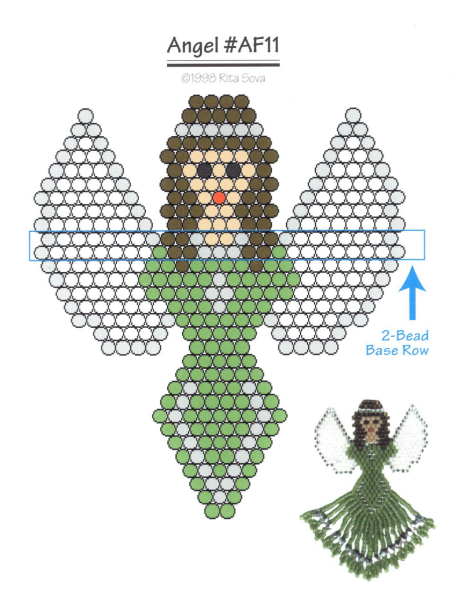

2-Bead Base Row

Fringe may be added to the dress bottom. I like a 9-1-6- (last 5 = turnaround) pattern. Start from the bottom center (down bead on right, add 9 green, 1-4mm silver, 6 green beads, go up 1st of last 6 added and continue up all remaining fringe beads and bead on left of brick stitch section). On the other 16 fringe you will follow above except, insert needle into same bead that thread is coming out of on brick-stitch section.

Angel #AM12

©1998 Rita Sova

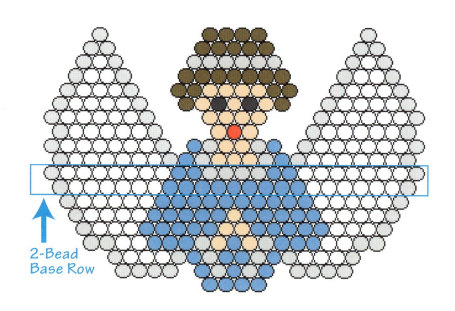

2-Bead Base Row

Angel #AF12

©1998 Rita Sova

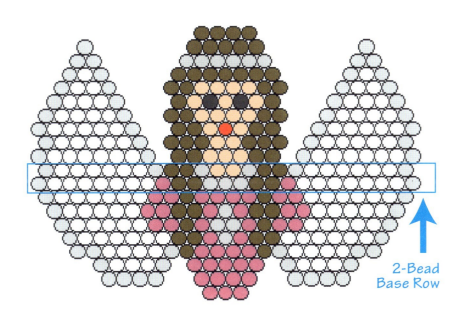

2-Bead Base Row

Angel #AM1
©1998 Rita Sova

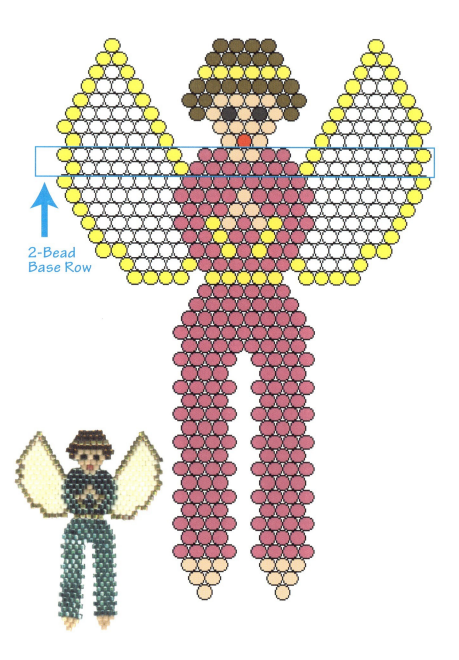

Angel #AM2
©1998 Rita Sova

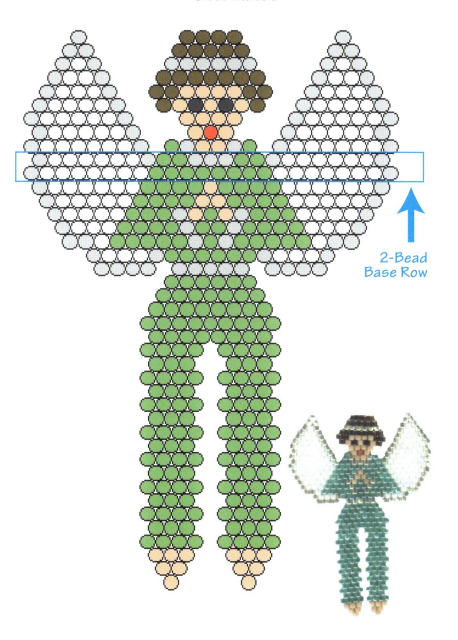

2-Bead Base Row

Angel #AM3

©1998 Rita Sova

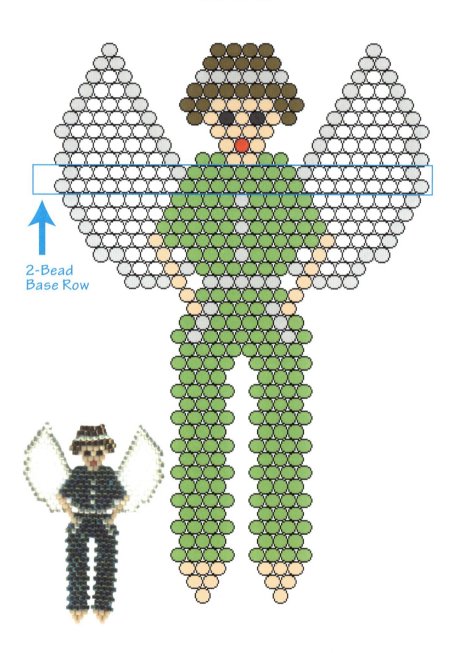

Angel #AM4
©1998 Rita Sova

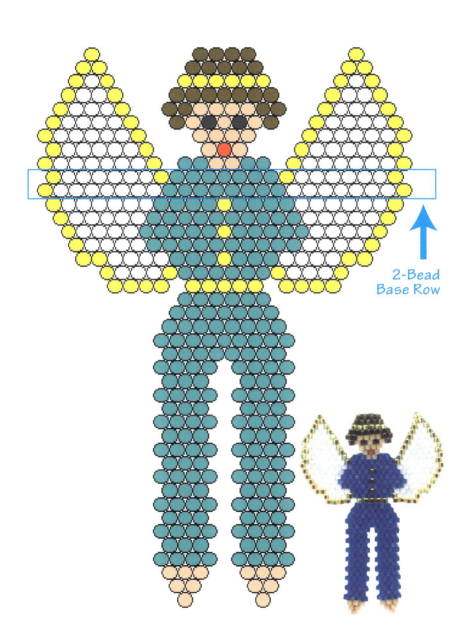

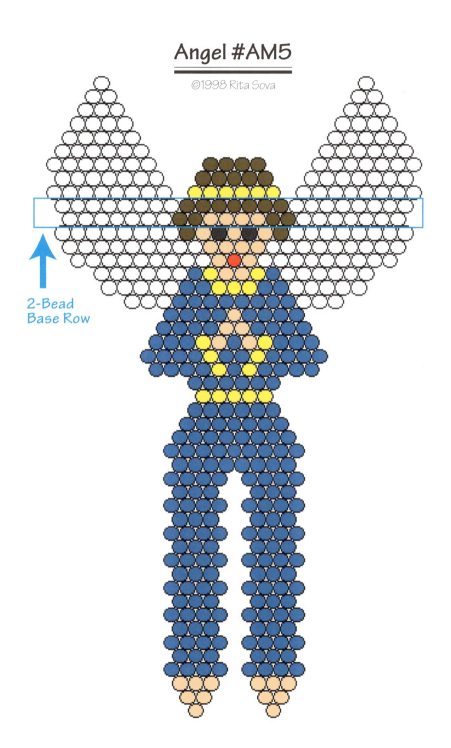

Angel #AM6

©1998 Rita Sova

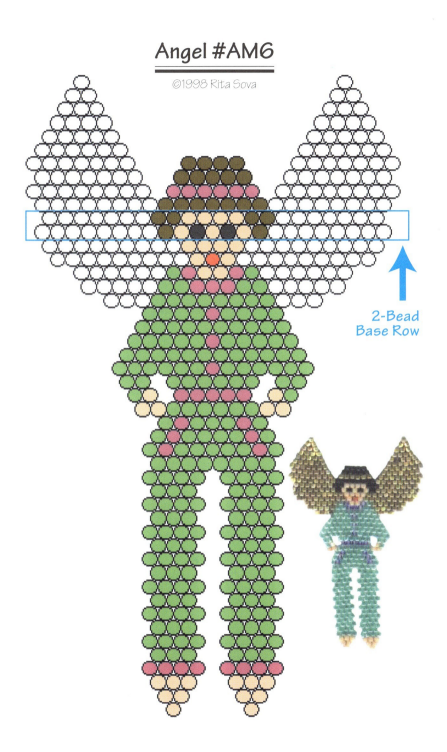

2-Bead Base Row

Angel #AM7

©1998 Rita Sova

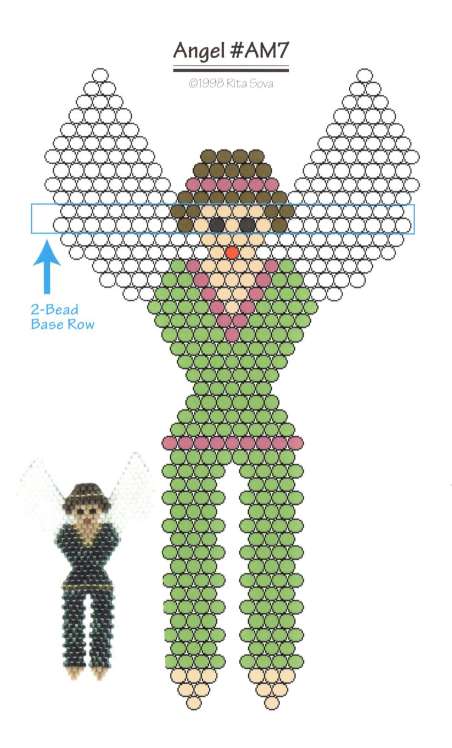

2-Bead Base Row

Angel #AM8
©1998 Rita Sova

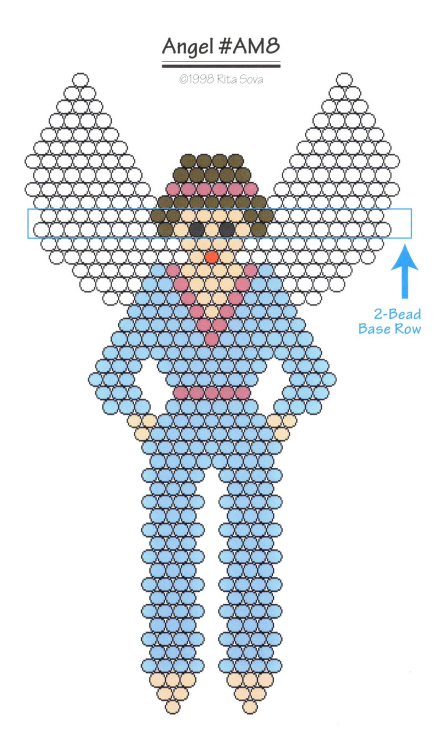

2-Bead Base Row

Angel #NAM1
©1998 Rita Sova

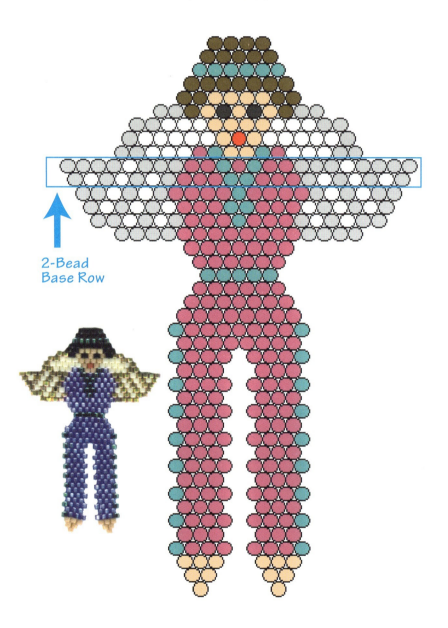

Angel #NAF1

©1998 Rita Sova

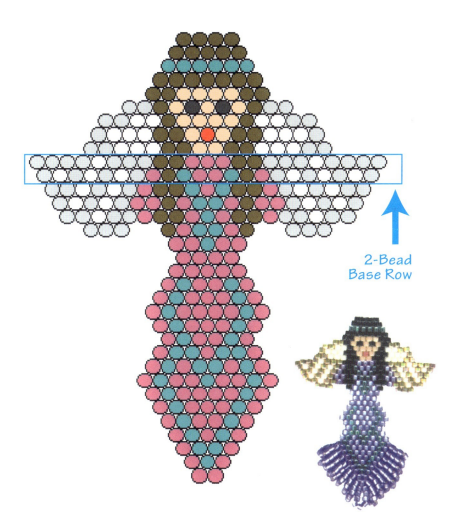

2-Bead Base Row

Fringe may be added to the female dress bottom. I like a 10-bead loop from the bottom center (down bead on right, add 10 beads, go up 1st of 10 added and bead on left). A 9-bead loop from each of the remaining 16 beads forming the bottom V. Out one bead, up the same bead after fringe beads are added.

Angel #NAM2
©1998 Rita Sova

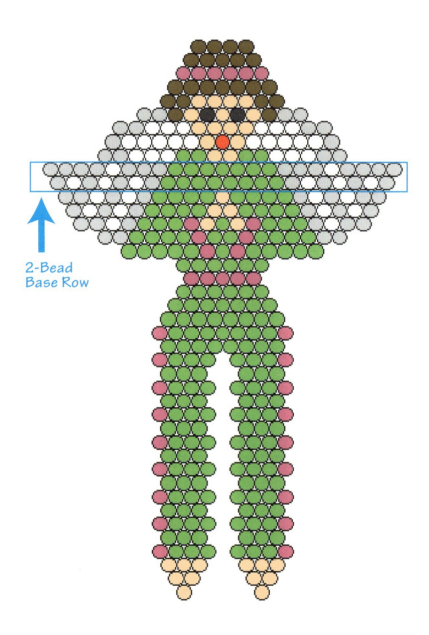

2-Bead Base Row

Angel #NAF2

©1998 Rita Sova

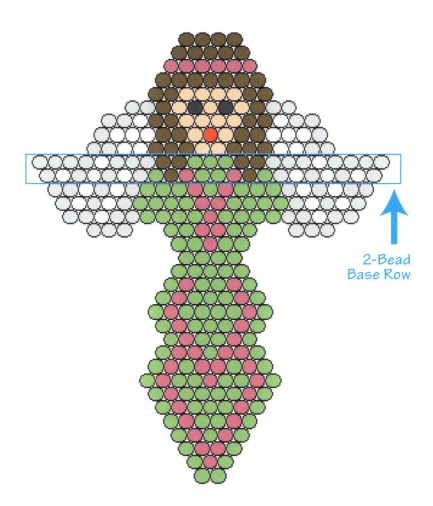

2-Bead Base Row

Fringe may be added to the female dress bottom. I like a 10-bead loop from the bottom center (down bead on right, add 10 beads, go up 1st of 10 added and bead on left). A 9-bead loop from each of the remaining 16 beads forming the bottom V. Out one bead, up the same bead after fringe beads are added.

Angel #NAM3

©1998 Rita Sova

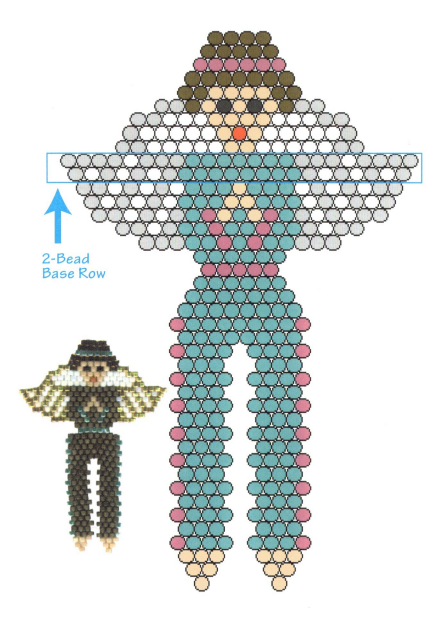

2-Bead Base Row

Angel #NAF3

©1998 Rita Sova

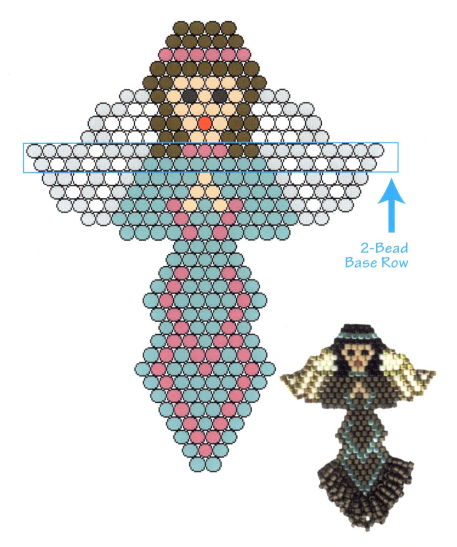

2-Bead Base Row

Fringe may be added to the female dress bottom. I like a 10-bead loop from the bottom center (down bead on right, add 10 beads, go up 1st of 10 added and bead on left). A 9-bead loop from each of the remaining 16 beads forming the bottom V. Out one bead, up the same bead after fringe beads are added.

Angel #NAM4

©1998 Rita Sova

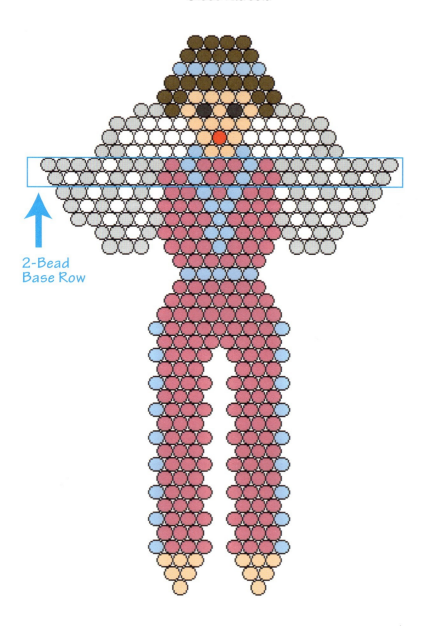

Angel #NAF4

©1998 Rita Sova

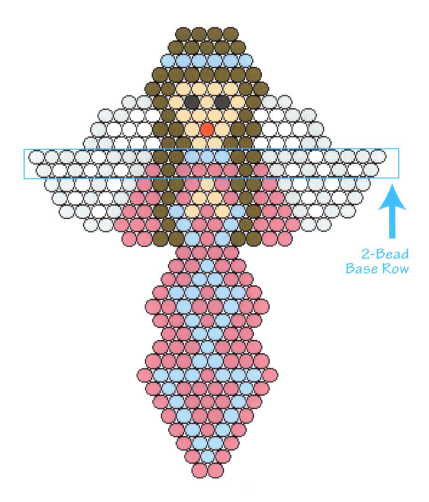

2-Bead Base Row

Fringe may be added to the female dress bottom. I like a 10-bead loop from the bottom center (down bead on right, add 10 beads, go up 1st of 10 added and bead on left). A 9-bead loop from each of the remaining 16 beads forming the bottom V. Out one bead, up the same bead after fringe beads are added.

Finishing items into Pins:

- Chose the size pin you want to use.
- I like to cover the backside of the metal pin with suede/pigskin. Cut a piece of soft suede or pigskin to a desirable shape, make sure there is enough to cover the pin back.
- Where ever you are going to use glue, I recommend you paint that area with clear nail polish (I use a base/topcoat) Use a medium amount of polish on the backside of item - always do a test spot first - some dyed beads will bleed, sometimes weird things happen. There is something about the nail polish that helps the glue adhere to the beads better.
- If needed cut slits or make a hole in the suede using an awl. Insert your pin and check position.
- Apply glue to the backside of the suede/pigskin and position over beads and press/smooth into place. (I like BOND 527)
- Let dry overnight. Keep in mind that however the item is positioned is the shape it will have when the glue is dry. Lay flat or prop into desired shape.